E. C. Ratcliff:

Reflections

on

Liturgical Revision

Edited by

David H. Tripp

*A Methodist Minister, serving in the Manchester (Cheetham Hill and Prestwich) Circuit
Secretary of the Henry Bradshaw Society*

GROVE BOOKS

BRAMCOTE   NOTTS.

CONTENTS

Introduction Copyright David H. Tripp 1980

The three essays Copyright Executor of E. C. Ratcliff

ACKNOWLEDGMENTS

The editor records his sincere thanks to:

Ratcliff's executor, Judge Curtis-Raleigh, for permission to reprint works of Ratcliff;

The Church Union for permission to reprint 'Principles of Liturgical Reform', and agreement with the printing of 'A Note on Schemes of Church Union';

The Revd. M. J. Butler, Communications Officer, Chichester Diocese, for agreement with the reprinting of 'The Communion Service of the Prayer Book';

The Trustees of S.P.C.K. and the Seabury Press for permission to quote from *The Lambeth Conference 1958: The Encyclical Letter* etc.

THE COVER PICTURE

is part of the original manuscript for the third essay in this Study, showing Ratcliff's distinctive handwriting (without corrections), it begins near the foot of page 28 below.

First Impression June 1980

ISSN 0306 0608

ISBN 0 905422 82 1

INTRODUCTION
by David Tripp

Ratcliff and Revision

Of the 51 published works associated with Ratcliff's name that are not reviews, at least eleven touch upon, or are devoted to, current debates about liturgical revision in the Church of England or involving the Church of England. Quite apart from his work on the coronation service for Queen Elizabeth II, he was engaged in three major projects of liturgical construction: in 'The Liturgy for India'[1], in the work of the Church of England Liturgical Commission from 1954 to 1967, and in the composition of the Ordinal in the Anglican-Methodist Unity Scheme. For one whose chief concerns were historical, and whose teaching responsibility committed him to work in research in many periods, this represents a considerable proportion of his effort.

A scholar whom he respected, and to whose memory he dedicated his study of the Old Syrian baptismal tradition, R. P. Casey, published in 1920 a paper entitled 'A Neglected Principle of Liturgical Revision' *(Harvard Theological Review,* XIII, 390-401), to the effect that many proposed liturgical amendments involve not only stylistic and devotional improvement but also unacknowledged doctrinal changes; the question of doctrine is primary, and must be decided openly. With this view Ratcliff entirely agreed; and he set similarly strict standards in the use of historical argument to support liturgical policy. He was especially concerned at the dangers implied by the readiness of authority to circumvent questions of truth:

> 'In the days of the Prayer Book controversy it was significant that [the] appeals [of the bishops] were less often made to sound learning than to the Holy Ghost.'[2]

His requirements for liturgical revisers were exacting:

> 'To compose a rite is easy enough; but to compose one well is the reverse of easy, as many essays at liturgical composition prove. If the composers are not to fail, first they must know precisely what they are setting out to do, and then they must know how to do it; that is to say, they must know the basic principles and notions, the essential meaning and content of their rite, and they must possess a knowledge, to be acquired only by wide and careful study, of the many and diverse ways in which what they seek to do has already been done.'

This dictum appears in a favourable review of the South India Ordinal[3], itself the work of a team whose criteria of liturgical learning were such that they could call themselves 'liturgically illiterate'.[4] Not all liturgical proposals

---

[1] The 1923 order was lightly revised in 1943; more substantially revised in 1948; published as *The Indian Liturgy* (Bombay; OUP; 1948); finally reprinted as 'A Liturgy for India' in *A Proposed Prayer Book . . . of the Church of India, Pakistan, Burma, and Ceylon . . .* (Madras, Delhi, Lahore; SPCK; 1952), pp.787-824.

[2] *The Menace of the Church Assembly* (1931), p.12.

[3] *Theology* Vol. LXIII, pp.7-15.

[4] A. Marcus Ward, in his *Pilgrim Church.*

met with such approval. The *York Revised Service for the Public Baptism of Infants* of 1951 he severely censured, not only because it failed to reflect the lessons of historical research, but more because it confused the picture of the Christian faith to be learned from it by worshippers and because its lack of clarity of expression and feebleness of language made it pastorally ineffective.

1. 'The Communion Service of the Prayer Book. Its Intention, Interpretation and Revision' (1935)

The Prayer Book crisis of 1927-8 did not mark the end of the campaign for and against the reshaping of Anglican worship. 1935, which saw the publication of Henry de Candole's *The Church's Offering* and of A. S. Duncan-Jones' *Why Change the Communion Service?*, also witnessed a flurry of liturgical controversy in the pages of the *Chichester Diocesan Gazette*. Ratcliff, moved by correspondence in church newspapers, wrote the article with the above title, which appeared in the January number of the *Gazette* (pp.7-12). This provoked considerable reaction:

(a) in the February edition:

 pp.52-5: a rejoinder by the Bishop Suffragan of Lewes (Hugh Maudslay Hordern) to the effect that Ratcliff was describing the structure of Cranmer's rite only, and not Anglican eucharistic doctrine; no one should presume to say what the Eucharist was not; and if the rite did not say all that you wanted, there were always hymns to fill the gaps.

 pp.56-63: a serious attack by Dr. C. H. Smyth, which must be analysed separately.

 pp.70-1: a letter from F. Keeling Scott, quoting Cosin the reviser of 1661/2 as a witness to Ratcliff's interpretation.

(b) in the March edition:

 pp.102-8: Ratcliff's reply to Smyth (reprinted here pp.16-19).

 p.116: a letter from Canon Samuel Bickersteth, supporting Bishop Hordern on the value of hymns as 'liturgical interpolations'.

 pp.116-8: an important letter of Norman Sykes, chiefly defending Ratcliff (and by implication severely rebuking Smyth) on the use of documents.

 p.118: a letter from 'M' to the same effect.

(c) in the April edition:

 p.161: a short rejoinder from Smyth.

Smyth's critique is already reflected in Ratcliff's reply, which meets it, for the most part, point by point. Smyth objects to,

(i) Ratcliff's method of taking documents literally, as if they were legal evidence (Ratcliff did not reply directly to this, but Sykes did it for him).

(ii) the suggestion that the rite is designed to express the mind of Cranmer: surely it is intended to express the mind of Christ?—and Smyth goes on to say (p.57):

 '... it does not follow that a Service which is an entirely adequate expression of what Cranmer thought in 1551 is necessarily an entirely adequate expression of the intention of Our Lord himself, or even of what the Church of England (which presumably has not been destitute of the guidance of the Holy Spirit since Cranmer's martyrdom) is thinking in 1935.'

(iii) the statement that the Anglican rite cannot be reconciled with the 'historic liturgies', since it is (he says) the lineal descendant of the Sarum Mass, and the 1549 service, which is the norm, also includes an Oriental feature.

(iv) Ratcliff's reading of Cranmer's theology.

(v) the notion that Cranmer's views give the only legitimate interpretation of the 1662 book. The 1559 and 1661/2 changes were, he says, not slight; and, in a fine passage which is supported by the close of Sykes' letter, remarks:

'. . . . in studying any liturgy, it is not sufficient to know its origins; you have also to account for its survival' (p.61).

Ratcliff's reply takes up three points: (iv), (v), and (ii). He does not give a detailed answer, and does not expose the fundamental misunderstanding of which Smyth was guilty. Ratcliff's original point was that many—indeed, all—of the proposed changes to the 'Prayer of Consecration' were based on a misreading of the whole character of the 1552 rite (and of its later forms). Ratcliff was applying one of the criteria for liturgical revision advocated by Bishop Frere in his *Some Principles of Liturgical Reform* (London, 1911), namely, congruity with the idea of worship embodied in the rite to be revised or enriched (pp.12-15). Even Frere, however, thought of the three prayers in 1552, and especially of the 'Prayer of Consecration' and the Prayer of Oblation, as belonging together and as being capable of reassembly (*op. cit.* 186-94). A similar, but more subtle, view is found in J. H. Srawley's *The English Consecration Prayer* (London, 1923). One supporter of the 1927 book who liked the newly reassembled prayer—but because it seemed to favour his brand of receptionism—was Bishop Headlam.[1] All these approaches, as Ratcliff saw, were mistaken in their assumption that the 'Prayer of Consecration' alone explains the essence of Cranmer's rite. The ground-plan of the whole service expresses a comprehensive theology, which will continue to come through to worshippers if the whole structure is not replaced.

Ratcliff came to amplify and modify his interpretation of Cranmer's rite. As Sykes had pointed out, it was not so phrased as to bind all its users to Cranmer's view of the presence, and, as Srawley had noted (pp.22-27), the prominence of the Words of Institution left room for a Lutheran view—and others. Ratcliff himself was to clarify the English tradition of consecration in terms of the Augustinian principle of adding the Word to the element[2], and spoke appreciatively of the way in which the 1662 book had served to remind Anglicans that they were part of the Church Catholic.[3] However, he maintained his view of the theory of oblation built into the English rite, and also his conviction that the traditional Catholic concept of eucharistic sacrifice called for a totally new rite.

[1] A. C. Headlam, *The New Prayer Book* (London 1927), pp.68-81.
[2] In *Theology*, Vol. LX, pp.229-236 and 273-280.
[3] As, e.g., in his preface to Cambridge University Press's Tercentary edition of B.C.P.

Smyth clearly assumed that Ratcliff wanted Anglicans to agree with Cranmer—quite wrongly; but his worst misreading of Ratcliff was his suspicion that he had no interest in our Lord's intention at the Supper. Ratcliff's review in the same volume of the *Gazette* (pp.361-2), where the dominical prayer asserted to be the indisputable model for Christian practice is characterized as 'Thanksgiving', shows clearly both his concern for Christ's intentions and also the way in which his researches were leading him to see the anaphora as an essentially 'purely eucharistic prayer', a matter on which he is still misunderstood.[1]

2. 'Principles governing Liturgical Reform' (1958)

The two remaining pieces require less commentary. The Church of England Liturgical Commission had been created in 1955. Its first achievement was the report *Prayer Book Revision in the Church of England* (S.P.C.K., London, 1957), of which Ratcliff was a signatory. This booklet surveyed events since the debacle of 1927, and noted what was going on throughout the Anglican Communion. Revision must meet the needs of Anglican unity; at home, it must be: conservative, faithful to Scripture but using the Church's proper liberty, expressive of sound contemporary insights into the Gospel; intelligible; contemporary but not trendy; acceptable to the main streams of Anglican thought; 'prayable', and supremely aimed at a more worthy worship of God.

Ratcliff's address to the 1958 Eucharistic Congress did not traverse the same ground. Here he speaks as a liturgical historian trying to meet the needs of people, especially young people, who sense an urgent need for new life in Christian worship. Right understanding of worship calls for an appreciation of the plan implicit in the beginnings of worship, and of the developments, sound and unsound, from that beginning. As in the early days, a missionary Church needs solid instruction, truly corporate life, awareness of unity with the Church triumphant. This calls for worship that is vigorously objective, centred upon the cross and resurrection of Christ. These are present in the Church, in concrete action, by which the Church gives thanks, bringing with it the only offering it has, Christ's self-oblation. Ratcliff's programme of liturgical revision as here set out extends only to the Eucharist. It was work on the Eucharist that led to Ratcliff's decision, after the form of Series 2 which he had helped to contruct had been seriously altered in the anamnesis-oblation, to resign from the Commission in 1967. By that time, the nature of the Commission's work had in any case been radically changed by the need to devise alternative services in modern English, which meant more than linguistic changes, as

---

1 The review is of Duncan-Jones' *Why Change the Communion Service?*. Interesting to note that ECR rejects an epiclesis chiefly as being extraneous to a prayer which is essentially a thanksgiving, and secondarily as being alien to modern Christian thought. For continued misunderstanding of ECR's view of the Anaphora as *thanksgiving*, cf Macomber on *Addai and Mari* in *Ephemerides Liturgicae* for 1978. ECR's account of the discrepancy between Anglican rite and s ome Anglican theology is supported in Addleshaw's *High Church Tradition* (London, 1941), and was taken up, with typical overstatement, in Dix's *Shape of the Liturgy* (Westminster, 1945). Dix never began to understand justification by faith, and never really tried.

can be seen from the speeches of R. C. D. Jasper and Stella Brook at the conference on liturgical reform in 1966.[1]

3. 'A Note on Schemes of Union, the Ministry and Forms of Ordination' (1959)

This paper, hitherto existing only in duplicated form, was prepared for a conference of the theological committee of the Church Union on the Lambeth Unity report, held on 7 January 1959.

The Church of South India, on the Ordinal of which Ratcliff was later to report so favourably, had been formed in 1947. By the time the 1958 Lambeth Conference met, two other major schemes of union were being debated: the *Scheme for Church Union in Ceylon,* and the *Plan of Church Union in North India and Pakistan.* The Committee on Church Unity and the Church Universal examined the progress of these two sets of negotiations (*The Lambeth Conference 1958 . . . with the Resolutions and Reports* (S.P.C.K., London and Seabury, Greenwich, 1958) 2.28-40). Their comments on the liturgical aspects of the projects are as follows (2.36-40):

2. THE SERVICES FOR THE UNIFICATION OF THE MINISTRY

The Committee has noted the *desire* and *intention* of the Negotiating Committees to provide a ministry 'fully accredited in the eyes of all their members, and so far as may be of the Church throughout the world', and is deeply concerned that the actual methods proposed by the Negotiating Committees should not fail to carry out that intention adequately.

The Services by which unification is to be achieved have a crucial importance. The Lambeth Conference of 1948 strongly recommended that unification at or near the start should be a part of every future scheme of union. The services proposed in the *Plan* and the *Scheme* are the first to be put forward to achieve such initial unification. For Anglicans future advance in reunion schemes depends greatly upon whether the services proposed can be considered sufficient and satisfactory for their purpose. It is necessary therefore to examine them carefully to see that the liturgical function and form is appropriate and is expressed in sufficiently clear phraseology.

All the negotiating Churches are agreed as to the functions which are to be fulfilled through the liturgical forms proposed. They are three:

1. Negatively, the liturgical form must be such as to raise no question as to the relative sufficiency, reality, or effectiveness of the various ministries which are brought to be unified.

2. Positively, the liturgical form must be one appropriate to the essential function of seeking from God through prayer and laying-on of hands a continuance and increase of spiritual gifts already received and possessed by each Minister, for the work of the Office and Order of Ministry in the Church of God to which he is now freshly called in the United Church.

3. In order that the intention of removing all ground for doubts or scruples may be fulfilled, the liturgical form must also be appropriate for its function of seeking from God that he will "endue each according to his need" with whatever of grace, gifts, character or authority may in the sight of God be needed for the Office and Order of Ministry referred to. Thus every Church may be satisfied that all of its inheritance has been faithfully conveyed to and shared by the ministry of the United Church.

It is clearly the earnest desire of all the negotiating Churches equally that these three functions may be fulfilled to the satisfaction of all, in order that the United Church may rejoice in a ministry possessed of the richness of all the Uniting Churches.

1 *Some Basic Principles* (S.P.C.K., London, 1966).

The Committee is happy to find that the first two of the three functions are abundantly fulfilled. It is its duty to examine with special care what is provided for the discharge of the third function, since the Anglican Communion as well as the negotiating Churches themselves would wish to be assured that no room for doubt or scruple is left there.

The form taken by the services for the unification of the ministries is as follows: Preface; Prayer; Laying-on of hands with Formula invoking the Holy Spirit.

In Anglican Ordinals, the Prayer in this position, while referring generally to ministries given by Christ to his Church, does not name the particular ministry which is being conferred. The Laying-on of hands is associated with the subsequent Formula in which the particular office or Order (Bishop/Priest in the Church of God) is explicitly named. The Committee appreciates the fact that the order of the *Plan* or *Scheme* is that of our own existing rites, and notes that the wording of the proposed Formula adds an element essential to this particular and unique form of unification of ministries. The Committee desires to make only two general comments before turning to consider the services of the *Plan* and the *Scheme* separately.

1. Wherever it is possible, it is desirable that in the Prayer (as well as in the Formula) the specific office or Order of Ministry in view should be named. Thereby an extra degree of precision and clarification is achieved.

2. In the Prayer and in the Formula reference is naturally made both to ministry in the Church of God and to ministry in the particular Church (North Inida, Pakistan or Ceylon). It avoids confusion of thought, if these two ministries are kept in their suitable order throughout.
   There is the grace and authority of ministry in the Church of God, which each brings and which is to be continued and enriched by means of the Prayer, the laying-on of hands, and the Formula. All this is properly in the sphere of the Universal Church and takes precedence over all else. There is also the conferring of authority and jurisdiction within the local Church. There is nothing to prevent the universal and the local significance being closely associated provided that they are placed in their appropriate order in such a way as this:
   'For the exercise of the office (of Bishop/Presbyter) in the Church of God according to the constitution of the Church of . . .'
   or, more simply:
   'in the Church of God and within the Church of . . .'

With these two clarifications the Committee considers that in general the services would fully satisfy the third function which is to be required of the liturgical form. We now turn to the services proposed in the *Plan* and the *Scheme* respectively.

CHURCH OF NORTH INDIA/PAKISTAN
The Bringing Together of the Episcopates

The Committee strongly recommends that the unification of the Ministry as far as concerns the bishops should be completed in a single act, and suggests that if this is done representative ministers from all the uniting Churches should take part in the laying-on of hands. Would it be not only acceptable to the negotiating Churches but actually an increase of the significance of this episcopal unification if presbyteral representatives of all the uniting Churches thus took part in the laying-on of hands upon the bishops, sharing both in the prayers for the Holy Spirit, and in the conferring of authority to exercise the office of a bishop in the united Church?

The service should begin with the reading of the Preface followed by the Presentation of Bishops in a form similar to that on page 8 of the *Services Proposed for Use at The Inauguration.*

The Committee suggests also that the formula at the laying-on of hands should be conformed to the formula accompanying the laying-on of hands in the Representative Act of Unification of the Ministry (*Plan,* p.57, para. 18).

The Committee further recommends that the prayer on pages 5 and 6 be modified along these lines (*Plan*, p.54):

> O Almighty Father, Everlasting God . . . making perfect His Church; Continue, we beseech Thee, Thy blessing already granted to these Thy servants called this day to a fresh dedication to Thy service as Bishops and Chief Pastors of the Church Universal; and on all of them pour out Thy Holy Spirit to enrich each according to his need with grace and authority for the exercise of the office of a Bishop in the Church of God according to the constitution of the Church of North India/Pakistan, that they may ever be ready, &c.

The Representative Act of Unification of the Ministry

Liturgical function and form. The proposals of the *Plan* at this point are undoubtedly confusing, and the Committee finds it extremely awkward that the bishops whose episcopates have already been brought together in the previous Act should again be involved in the course of the same service in an Act which provides practically an identical prayer.

It is to be remembered first that the Churches have already been united in the first part of the service whereby the separate inheritances of the uniting Churches have come together in a single stream of Church life.

Then secondly the episcopates have been united with a specific mention of the office and ministry which is being so unified, in such a form as to remove all doubt or scruple.

The third step is entitled a representative act of unification of the ministry. The whole ministry of each Church had its part in the unifying of the Churches; the episcopate has been uinfied and commissioned by the joint action of bishops and presbyters, on the assumption that the suggestion made above has been accepted. What remains is to unify the presbyterate so as to complete the union in such a way as to bring spiritual enrichment to all and to remove at this level also all doubt or scruple. The unification at this level must be by laying-on of hands (including both episcopal and presbyteral hands) together with a prayer before it and with a formula accompanying it. In the prayer or in the formula or in both, the office and ministry to which the laying-on of hands is related must be mentioned, that is to say in this context the presbyterate. As the service stands, it is in fact very difficult to name this office in the prayer in such a way that it will not appear to include the bishops taking part in the representative act, while it would involve some element of confusion and even of insincerity to let it be taken indifferently as covering bishops and presbyters. It might look like mere repetition. That is why the Committee recommends that the unification of bishops should be completed in a single act. If the Committee's suggestions are adopted the presentation of the representatives of the ministry would not include bishops.

The Prayer would then be said by one of the bishops, and together with him representative ministers from each of the Churches now united should lay their hands on three ministers chosen beforehand, none of whom should be a bishop, using the form of words which the Committee has recommended for the unification of the episcopate. The bishop, together with the three chosen ministers, should lay hands on each of the representatives minister from each Church (except the bishop) using the same formula.

An alternative suggestion. While the Committee prefers the suggestion just made, it offers the following alternative suggestion:

The bishops should stand aside from the general statement to be made by all the other representatives of the Churches and from the prayer which precedes the laying-on of hands, seeing that in their case these have been already used, but not from the laying-on of hands.

> The laying-on of hands should be by the three chosen ministers (one of them being a bishop) and should be accompanied by the formula on page 9 (*Plan*, p.57, para. 18), with the omission, when hands are being laid on a bishop, of the words . . . 'mayst thou receive . . . within this Church; and . . .'

> In addition, for the reason stated on page 37, the prayer (pp.8-9) should be modified in some such way as follows:

>> Continue thy blessing already given and upon all thy servants called this day to a fresh dedication to thy service pour out thy Holy Spirit and endue each according to his need with grace and authority for the exercise of the ministry of a presbyter in the Church Universal within this Church of North India/ Pakistan.

CHURCH OF LANKA

Order of Service for the Unification of the Ministry

> For the reason given above (p.37), the Committee strongly recommends that in the Prayer for the Ministry (*Scheme*, pp.26-27) for the words 'presbyter in this Church of Lanka within the Church Universal' should be substituted the words 'presbyter in the Church Universal according to the Constitution of the Church of Lanka' (or, more simply, 'in the Church Universal and within the Church of Lanka'). A similar order of phrases should consistently be used in any formula which may follow. It may be noted that the suggested order of phrases is already used under item 13 in the Order of Service (p.24).

Ratcliff advised the Theological Committee of the Church Union on the liturgical and theological issues of ordination through these years, and his advserse report on the Lanka scheme (*Unification,* 1961) is another part of his contribution. At the time of his death, Ratcliff was actively participating in another proposed union scheme, between the Church of England and the Methodist Church of Great Britain, the Ordinal associated with this being largely his creation.

The memorandum now first printed begins with specific questions raised by the Ceylon and North India proposals, and goes on to the positive principles on which his last work was based.

Liturgical and other writings of E. C. Ratcliff

A. H. Couratin and the present editor have compiled a bibliography of Ratcliff's published writings, which has appeared as *Edward Craddock Ratcliff 1896-1967: A Bibliography of his Published Works* (Alcuin Club, London, 1972) and again, with additions, in the volume *E. C. Ratcliff: Liturgical Studies* edited by them (S.P.C.K., London, 1976), pp.1-10.

Since 1976, some further pieces have come to light, and are here listed for the convenience of students:

1923

E. C. Ratcliff with J. C. Winslow, D. R. Athavale, J. E. G. Festing *An Order for the Administration of the Holy Communion sanctioned by the Episcopal Synod of India for experimental use in the Diocese of Bombay in places selected by the Bishop of Bombay.* (Longmans, Green and Co., London).

(This is an adaptation of the rite printed in J. C. Winslow, ed., *The Eucharist in India,* 1920 (q.v.); although enjoying synodical authority, the revised form still appears over the names of its four authors also).

1931

'The Menace of the Church Assembly' (University Sermon, Cambridge, 31 May 1931), in *The Modern Churchman,* June 1931, also published separately (Basil Blackwell, Oxford).

1961

Unification. A Liturgical Analysis ('. . . correspondence on the subject of the proposals for unifying the ministry set out in the Scheme of Church Union in Ceylon . . .') (The Church Union, n.d., London).

1965

'The order of the Consecration of the Bp. of duresme the xxvii of July 1589. with a short commentary by E. C. Ratcliff' in *The Bishoprick,* Vol. 40 (1965), No. 4 (August), pp.84-89. (A subsequent number contained a note correcting an error in one of Radcliff's sources. Radcliff gratefully acknowledged the correction.)

At the end of the list could now be added the concluding piece in this collection, which has not previously been published:

1980

'A Note on Schemes of Union, the Ministry and Forms of Ordination' ('Paper contributed by Professor E. C. Ratcliff at a conference of the Theological Committee [sc., of the Church Union] on the Lambeth Unity Report, January 7th 1959'), in David Tripp (ed.) *E. C. Ratcliff: Reflections on Liturgical Revision* (Grove Liturgical Studies No. 22), pp.27-32.

1. THE COMMUNION SERVICE OF THE PRAYER BOOK
Its Intention, Interpretation and Revision[1]

I

For some weeks past certain church newspapers have been devoting space to correspondence, articles and reports of addresses on the revision of the central portion of the Communion Service in the Book of Common Prayer. By some it is held that the service would be improved by a re-arrangement of the prayers without any verbal alteration. Others press for a use of the Consecration Prayer in the revision of the Service proposed and rejected in 1927-28, in which we observe not only a re-arrangement of prayers, but considerable verbal change as well. Both these parties are agreed in treating the present service as sufficient in itself. Both are agreed, further, in stating that the changes they desire do not alter, but rather explicate, the doctrinal significance of the Service of 1662. Both are also agreed that the schemes of revision they favour would bring the existing Service into line with the historic liturgies of either 'the West' or 'the East'. In a word, whatever the differences between these two parties, they are agreed in implying, if they avoid definitely asserting, that the present Communion Service achieves its purpose in an unsatisfactory, or at least in an indifferent, manner. The present article is devoted to a consideration of this point.

The criterion of any rite or liturgical service is the adequacy with which it gives expression to its purpose or intention. The intention of the Communion Service, none can dispute, is the fulfilment of the Command *Do this in remembrance of me.* In this respect, it will be recognized the English Communion Service is at one with all other eucharistic offices whether reformed or unreformed. But what interpretation is to be placed upon the Command? The historic liturgies of West and East for the most part interpret the words as a command to make a formal verbal memorial before God of our Lord's passion and death, and to offer a sacrifice. *Wherefore, O Lord, we Thy servants . . . remembering the most blessed passion of the same Christ thy Son our Lord . . . offer to thy divine majesty of thine own gifts and presents a pure sacrifice . . . holy bread of eternal life and cup of everlasting salvation,* says the Canon of the Roman Mass after the words *As often as ye do this, ye shall do it in remembrance of me;* and in the Byzantine liturgy commonly attributed to S. John Chrysostom, after the words *Take, eat,* etc., and *Drink ye all of this,* etc., the celebrant is directed to say, *Therefore remembering this saving command and all that happened on our behalf, the cross, the tomb . . . we offer to Thee thine own of thine own.*

In the course of centuries conceptions of the Christian sacrifice have undergone development. When these Memorial—or Anamnesis—(to use the term current among liturgiologists) clauses first took form, the sacrifice was considered to be one of bread and wine. This conception is as old as Irenaeus, according to whom our Lord taught His disciples to offer bread and wine to God, 'not as though He were in need, but that they themselves might not be either unfruitful or unthankful.' Literally interpreted, the Byzantine Rite still offers a sacrifice of bread and wine, because its formula of consecration, *i.e.,* the Epiclesis, or petition for the change of the elements into Christ's Body and Blood by the operation of the Holy Spirit, is not recited

---

1 [*Chichester Diocesan Gazette,* Vol. XVI (1935), pp.7-12, 102-108. For an introduction to it, see p.4 above. The presentation of the original is retained.]

until after the Anamnesis has been said. In the Roman Mass, on the other hand, the Anamnesis is recited after the consecration is believed to have been effected by the saying of the words *This is my body, This is the cup of my blood.* It is therefore not difficult to understand how, wherever the Roman Mass was in use, the Christian sacrifice was conceived as the offering of the Body and Blood of our Lord, and how the Mass itself came to be regarded as in some sense a continuation or repetition of the sacrifice on the Cross. The Greek and Roman Churches may differ as to the form of consecration and as to the position of the consecration formula in their respective liturgies, but they are in accord as to the effect of consecration. They are in accord also as to the nature of the sacrifice offered in their liturgies, for whatever be the literal meaning of the Byzantine prayers, Greek theologians have been accustomed since the fifth century to regard the victim of the eucharistic sacrifice as identical with the Victim of the sacrifice on the Cross. The Mass and the Divine Liturgy alike are a commemoration before God of the Lord's passion and death, both by the words of the celebrant, and also by his offering of the 'gifts' in sacrifice, conformably, as it is believed, with the Lord's Command.

How is the Command interpreted in the English CommunionService? That Service, it will be remembered, is in substance the Communion Service of the Prayer Book of 1552; and to answer the question we must discover the correct interpretation of that office. There is no direct evidence as to who framed it; but, apart from contemporary references, a study of Cranmer's *Answer* to Bishop Gardiner's *Explication* of Catholic eucharistic doctrine leaves little doubt it was he. Gardiner's *Explication* had interpreted the English Mass of 1549 in terms of Catholic belief. Cranmer's *Answer,* published in 1551, foreshadowed the supersession of the English Mass by a service 'agreeable with the institution of Christ, with S. Paul, and the old primitive and apostolic church.'[1] 'The true use of the Lord's supper,' Cranmer writes, 'is to be restored again'[2]; and in Cranmer's account of that use we learn his interpretation of the Command. The true use, he asserts, is one 'wherein godly people assembled together may receive the sacraments every man for himself, to declare that he remembereth what benefit he hath received by the death of Christ.'[3] In other words, the purpose of the Communion Service is, not to make a memorial of Christ's death before God, but to recall it to the minds of Christian men. The true Anamnesis, therefore, is the act of communion, by which the worshipper receive bread and wine *in remembrance that Christ died for* them.

This interpretation, it will be noted, appears to make no room for a Catholic theory of consecration such as Gardiner held. Cranmer, in fact, definitely rejects such a theory. The consecration of the bread and wine is the separation of them to 'an holy use.'[4] The communicant receives bread and wine; but if he be duly prepared, his 'visible and corporal feeding' upon them is accompanied by a parallel feeding, invisible and spiritual, upon Christ's Flesh and Blood.[5] In the words of the Prayer Book, *receiving the creatures of bread and wine, according to Jesus Christ's holy institution, in remembrance of His death and passion,* the communicant is *made partaker*

1 *Works of Abp. Cranmer* (Parker Society, 1844) Vol. I., p.354.
2 *Ibid.,* p.349.
3 *ibid.* pp.349, 350.
4 *ibid.* p.177.
5 *ibid.* p.37.

of His most blessed Body and Blood. These words, it will be remembered, are drawn from a prayer to which Cranmer does not prefix the title, 'The Prayer of Consecration.' In the sixteenth century the term 'consecration' connoted ideas which the Reformers considered erroneous; and when the term was restored to use in the revision of 1662, it was employed by men who rejected the doctrine associated with it by theologians of the unreformed tradition.

With the rejection of the Catholic theory of consecration there followed inevitably the repudiation of the Catholic doctrine of the eucharistic sacrifice. Cranmer objected to this on two grounds. First, he argued, the sacrifice on the Cross was once and for all completed on the Cross, so that there is no future need for such sacrifice; and secondly, he maintained, the unreformed doctrine entails a misconception of the priest's function, in that it leads to the mistaken belief that in the Communion Service the priest alone can fulfil the Lord's Command. Here we encounter one of Cranmer's distinctive ideas. It is not the celebrant only, but each individual communicant, who fulfils, by his act of communion, the Lord's Command; similarly it is not the priest only, but each individual Christian, who offers to God the Christian sacrifice.[1] What, then, is the Christian sacrifice, as Cranmer understands it? It is the offering of 'laud, praise and thanksgiving,' whereby we 'testify our duties unto God, and shew ourselves thankful unto Him'; it is, at the same time, the oblation of ourselves, which 'we ourselves offer to God by Christ,' and which 'generally is our whole obedience unto God, in keeping His laws and commandments.' The Christian sacrifice, in short, is the Christian life, not a liturgical act, though capable of receiving liturgical expression.

To most readers of this article the ideas outlined in the preceding paragraphs will seem so commonplace as perhaps to merit impatience at a reiteration of them. Yet in most cases it is probably true that familiarity with these ideas does not proceed from acquaintance with the treatise of Cranmer under review, but is due to knowledge of another document. That document is the Communion Service of the Prayer Book, in which the ideas of the *Answer* find ordered liturgical expression in perfect logical sequence. In other words, the *Answer* gives us the true interpretation of the Communion Service. The central portion of the Service opens with the third Exhortation, to be said when the communicants are *'conveniently placed for the receiving of the Holy Sacrament.'* In the third Exhortation, now nearly always omitted but nevertheless integral to the Prayer Book liturgy, we may discern the scheme of thought underlying the portion of the Service which is to follow. Repentance, confession, absolution and the *lively faith* re-kindled by the Comfortable Words lead on to the thanksgiving of the Preface. Thence, after the Prayer of Humble Access, we pass to the solemn recollection of the sacrifice of the Cross and of the institution of the Sacrament in remembrance of it. Immediately, in natural and appropriate sequence and by no abrupt transition, there follows the fulfilment of the purpose of the institution in the solemn act of remembrance on the part of priest and people. This is the receiving of communion, which, because it is central in, and is the *raison d'être* of, the Rite, gives its name to the whole Service. The remembrance of the Lord's death and passion on our behalf, *that he might make us the children of God,* lends peculiar fitness at this

1 *ibid.* pp.345–367. See F. C. Burkitt, *Eucharist and Sacrifice*, ed. 1927, pp.24ff.

moment to the common praying of the Lord's Prayer. Then, still in remembrance of the death and passion, and in a consciousness of sonship deepened by their saying of the Son's prayer to their Father, the communicants can proceed to do that which before communion would have seemed inappropriate and out of place. By the words of the celebrant, they now offer their *sacrifice of praise and thanksgiving,* and make the oblation of themselves, both *souls and bodies.* This is the only sacrifice which the English Service recognizes; and it will be observed that we have here a sequence recalling that of the older rite, in which the institution-narrative is followed by the Anamnesis, which itself, as we have seen, is consummated by the offering of the sacrifice. For those to whom sacrificial suggestions in this Service are distasteful, the alternative post-communion prayer provides for the expression of thanksgiving and of aspiration to self-dedication in language of non-sacrificial import. With the Great Doxology, prescribed perhaps in imitation of the singing of a hymn at the end of the Last Supper, and with the Blessing, the Service reaches its close. The slight additions made to the Service in 1559 and 1662 have in no way altered its balance or character. The re-employment of the term 'consecration,' so we have noticed already, was not intended as an abandonment of reformed theory. The restoration of the manual acts, and of the Words of Administration used in the Mass of 1549, reminiscent as they are of the acts and words of Christ at His Supper, serve only to render more vivid the remembrance which the worshippers are present to make.

Enough has now been said to show that, whatever objections may be brought against the English Communion Service, it cannot be condemned as imperfectly achieving its purpose. Its intention is expressed not merely with adequacy, but with a completeness and grandeur that injudicious revision might easily damage. The schemes of revision, desired by the two parties to whom reference was made at the beginning of this article, argue in those who propose them a failure to understand the character and purpose of the Communion Service. That Service is *sui generis.* In its interpretation of the Dominical Command, in its conception of worship, and in its liturgical structure, it is not, and was not designed to be, parallel with any historic liturgy of West or East. To judge it by the historic litiurges and to attempt to bring it into line with them is to submit it to a criterion which is irrelevant and inapplicable. It may be that those who desire revision prefer the conceptions of worship embodied in or associated with the ancient Latin and Greek liturgies, and hope, by the means they propose, to secure expression for these conceptions in the Communion Service. But from the account of them in this article, it will perhaps be clear that the ancient conceptions of worship and sacrifice are incompatible with those of the reformed English Rite. A form of revision, whether of Roman or Greek type, which expresses, either wholly or in part, the conceptions of the ancient liturgies, so far from explicating the significance of the present Service, cannot but destroy it. The aim of the revisers, in fine, can only be secured, not through the revision of the existing Order, but through the substitution for it of a different Rite.

[The January 1935 article finished here. Charles Smyth replied in February 1935 (see pp.4-5 above). Ratcliff responded again in March 1935, as follows.]

II

The article by Mr. Charles Smyth, under the title above, in the February number of the *Diocesan Gazette,* in comment upon an article of my own with the same title, calls for some reply both on account of the intrinsic interest and importance of the subject in dispute between us, and also because of the accusation of blunder or disingenuousness which he brings against me. Accusations of this description, though once among the conventions of ecclesiastical controversy, are, presumably, no longer so, and are not intended to be treated as mere formalities. The ideal method of an answer to Mr. Smyth would be that pursued by Archbishop Cranmer in his *Answer to a Crafty and Sophistical Cavillation devised by Stephen Gardiner.* This method would further have a peculiar appropriateness in view of the subject of our controversy; but it would too soon exhaust both space in the *Gazette* and patience in its readers, so that a shorter treatment must necessarily be adopted.

Mr. Smyth's main points against me are (i) that I have improperly related Cranmer's *Answer* to the Prayer Book of 1552; (ii) that I have attempted, again improperly, to restrict the meaning of the Communion Service to the meaning which Cranmer intended it to bear; and (iii) that I have evaded discussing whether or not our present Communion Service adequately expresses the mind of Christ, and this, says Mr. Smyth, is the point at issue.

What Mr. Smyth has to say about Cranmer's *Answer* and its incorporation of his *Defence of the True and Catholic Doctrine of the Sacrament of the Body and Blood of Christ* was already known to me. Both the *Defence* and the *Answer* were before me as I wrote; and I quoted from the *Defence* as it is used in the *Answer,* because Cranmer's controversy with Gardiner seems to me to have given the *Defence* a new significance. I was also aware that the reference in both *Defence* and *Answer* was to the Communion Service of 1549; if Mr. Smyth will do me the honour of glancing again at my composition he will see that I have made no statement to the contrary. Having stated that the *Answer* was published in 1551 (p.13), *i.e.,* when the Service of 1549 was still in force, I later stated (p.14) that 'the *ideas* of the *Answer* find ordered liturgical expression in perfect logical sequence' in the existing Communion Service, and concluded that 'the *Answer* gives us the true interpretation of the Communion Service.' If Mr. Smyth would prefer it, I am ready to say that the *Defence* gives us that interpretation. But there still remains a difference between what I wrote and Mr. Smyth's interpretation of it.

Mr. Smyth's principal objection, however, is to my statement that the *Answer* 'foreshadowed the supersession of the English Mass' by the Service of 1552, and he proceeds to discuss the statement as though in place of 'foreshadowed', I had written 'foretold.' 'Foretold' would admittedly have been a blunder. In my defence I must call attention to a not unimportant point which Mr. Smyth neglects in his account of the controversial writings of Gardiner and Cranmer (p.58). In the *Explication* Gardiner maintained, not only that 'catholic' teaching concerning the Sacrament was set forth in the Prayer Book of 1549, but that Cranmer's own doctrine, although Cranmer 'doth after specially allow' the Book (which Gardiner treated as Cranmer's work), was nevertheless at variance with it. 'All the sum of his teaching doth improve it in that point. So much is he contrary to himself in this work.'[1] Cranmer in his *Answer* set out to shew that the

---

[1] *Works of Abp. Cranmer.* Parker Society, Vol. I., p.71.

teaching of the Prayer Book was in conformity with his own rather than with Gardiner's. Whether or not the Mass of 1549 was deliberately promulgated as an 'interim rite,' as Bucer and Fagius appear to have understood when they visited Cranmer in April 1549[1], or whether or not Cranmer himself was entirely satisfied with his *Answer,* it was made clear to him by Gardiner's treatise that the true doctrine of the Sacrament, as the Archbishop understood it, was not insured by the then Prayer Book. If the true use of the Lord's Supper were to be restored again it could not be by the Mass of 1549 which Gardiner had successfully interpreted in catholic terms; it must be restored by another form of service. Gardiner's *Explication* had been written in 1550, although it was not printed until 1551. It had been presented to Cranmer by Gardiner at his trial in December, 1550. Cranmer answered it in 1551. Already in January of that year liturgical changes were on the way, as we may learn from a letter written by Peter Martyr to Martin Bucer, in which a statement to that effect is made on the authority of Cranmer himself.[2] These changes issued in the Prayer Book of 1552.

The Communion Service of the Book of 1552 was, in the words of Mr. Smyth, 'a carefully revised and, if you will, a mutilated edition of 'the English Mass of 1549''.' The mutilations are significant: they consist in the removal of whatever in the Rite of 1549 Gardiner had interpreted as 'agreeable to the Catholic Doctrine.' Further, the use of the vestments was discontinued, and the altar became the communion table. The Communion Service of 1552 was, in effect, a second answer to Gardiner. Unlike the Mass of 1549 it was not at variance with the true doctrine as Cranmer had stated it in his *Defence.* Mr. Smyth writes that 'it is the 1549 rite and not that of 1552, which is the basis of Cranmer's exposition of Eucharistic doctrine in the *Defence.*' To one who had not read the *Defence* these words would suggest that the work was a conscious commentary on the Service of 1549. That is not the case; and I can hardly believe that Mr. Smyth intended to convey the suggestion. I hesitate to differ from so eminent an authority as he is; yet I am bound to say that a re-reading of he *Defence* confirms me in the opinion in which I wrote my article, that in the *Defence* Cranmer's intention was to set out what he considered to be correct views about the Holy Communion and that his concern with the Service of 1549 was incidental, as his references to it were incidental, and also few. In short, the work is what it purports to be, a defence of a doctrine and not of a rite. Further, Mr. Smyth has said nothing to make me change my opinion that, when Cranmer saw that these views were not safeguarded by the Service of 1549 he was concerned to change not his views, but the Service, although circumstances required him to defend the Service in his *Answer;* and also that, when in the *Answer* he copied from the *Defence* the passages to my use of which Mr. Smyth objects, those passages had for Cranmer at least a new significance, in that, though he did not delete his few and incidental allusions to the then existing Service, change had already been decided upon and that Service was doomed. This opinion, I submit, is not untenable in the light of the evidence presented in Mr. Smyth's *Cranmer and the Reformation under Edward VI.*

1 See Gasquet and Bishop, *Edward VI and the Book of Common Prayer* 2 pp.234-5.
2 See Mr. Smyth's *Cranmer and the Reformation under Edward VI.,* p.246.

I have now to consider Mr. Smyth's second point against me. He objects that I attempt to limit the meaning of our present Communion Service to that which can be found for it in Cranmer's *Answer* or *Defence*. He points out that a document can mean what it says, rather than what its author intended it to mean, and that it can therefore mean more than its author meant. With this principle I cannot quarrel: but I am not in agreement with Mr. Smyth in his application of it in this instance. A document may well mean more than it was intended to mean; can it, however, be made to mean what it was intended not to mean?

'Cranmer's liturgy has survived,' writes Mr. Smyth, 'only because it admits, and indeed invites, a more Catholic interpretation than that which he himself would have desired to put upon it.' Mr. Smyth, I note, does not appear to dispute my account of the interpretation which Cranmer intended his liturgy to have. As an example of a more catholic interpretation he refers me to the *Responsio* sent to Pope Leo XIII. by the Abps. of Canterbury and York in 1897, rebuking me for 'conveniently ignoring it. It would be an impertinence to comment upon the great learning of the [Abps'.] *Responsio;* it would also be impossible to deny that the teaching of the Abps. on the Eucharistic sacrifice represents a permissible opinion within the Church of England. But is the opinion permitted by the Communion Service itself? It is noteworthy that when the Abps. allude to Eucharistic consecration—they speak of 'consecrating the gifts already offered that they may become to us the Body and Blood of our Lord Jesus Christ'[1]—their language is suggestive of the rite of 1549 rather than of that of 1552 or 1662. In their interpretation of the Communion Service, the Abps. say 'We plead and represent before the Father the sacrifice of the cross.'[2] These words are reminiscent neither of the rite of 1549 nor of the present Service. They are covered, however, by the anamnesis clause of the rite of 1549. There is no sentence in the present Service, on the other hand, which expresses the thought contained in the Abps'. statement. According to the Exhortations in the Communion Service, the sacrifice of the cross is rather represented before us. *I purpose . . . to administer to all such as shall be religiously and devoutly disposed the most comfortable Sacrament of the Body and Blood of Christ; to be by them received in remembrance of his meritorious Cross and Passion,* we read in the First Exhortation. In the Second are words of similar tenor: *as the son of God did vouchsafe to yield up his soul by death upon the Cross for your salvation; so it is your duty to receive the Communion in remembrance of the sacrifice of his death, as he himself hath commanded.* The Third Exhortation echoes the thought: *And to the end that we should always remember the exceeding great love of our Master and only Saviour Jesus Christ, thus dying for us . . .; he hath instituted and ordained holy mysteries, as pledges of his love, and for a continual remembrance of his death, to our great and endless comfort.* The same thought is brought out in the more familiar exordium of the Prayer of Consecration. It will not, I hope, be disrespectful if I suggest that the Abps.' *Responsio* interprets the Service of 1662 in the sense of that of 1549. The practice is common nowadays; and it might not be unjustifiable, if the history of English liturgical revision had been other than it is. But when the differences between the rites of 1549 and 1552 and the significance of these differences have been taken into account, it is impossible to interpret the latter rite, either in its original form or in that of 1662, as if those

1 See the translation in *Anglican Orders*. S.P.C.K. p.35.   2 *ibid.*

differences did not exist. If we so interpret it, we are not merely making the document mean more than it was intended to mean; we are making it mean what we know it was intended not to mean, and what it cannot be made to mean, without considerable display of that kind of ingenuity which has brought theological argument into distrust. That the Prayer Book Communion Service is, in fact, *sui generis* and that it cannot successfully be made to bear the sort of interpretation which the Abps.' *Responsio* would put upon it is favoured by several considerations. Whenever Anglicans who have professed the more catholic interpretation of the Communion Service have had the opportunity, they have abandoned it as it stands. Either they have re-arranged its central section and incorporated into it passages from the rite of 1549, as in the case of the Scottish Liturgies of 1637, 1743 and later; or, while following the main lines of the clauses of consecration and oblation in the rite of 1549, they have expressed the eucharistic oblation in more definite phraseology, as in the rite of the Province of South Africa. Certain of the Nonjurors went as far as to devise an entirely new rite. In England, where the use of the Prayer Book remains obligatory, the revival of catholic beliefs during the last century has led to the practice of farcing the central section of the Communion Service with paragraphs from the Canon of the Roman Mass. If the present Communion Service can successfully be made to bear a more catholic interpretation than Cranmer intended to give it, it is difficult to account for such deviations from, and alterations in, the Service, as these. They cannot easily be reconciled with Mr. Smyth's contention.

The third of Mr. Smyth's objections to my article causes me some wonder. He takes me to task for not considering the point at issue, which he says, 'is not whether our present rite adequately expresses the mind of Cranmer, but whether it adequately expresses the mind of Christ.' Later, quoting my own words, 'The intention of the Communion Service, none can dispute, is the fulfilment of the Command, Do this in remembrance of me,' he comments, 'Precisely: that is the issue. And E.C.R. displays considerable ingenuity in evading it.' So also, I may observe, does Mr. Smyth. My purpose in writing my article was to discuss the intention and interpretation of the Communion Service, and to indicate its difference in this respect from the historic liturgies. My protest was made against a disregard of this difference, and against proposals to revise the Communion Service in such a way as to confuse reformed and unreformed conceptions of the Service. It lay outside my field to discuss whether one or other of these conceptions expressed the mind of Christ or no. It need hardly be said that framers of liturgies, reformed and unreformed alike, believed their forms to express the mind of Christ: the same is true, presumably, of those who use them. The passages from the Communion Service to which I have referred in this article can leave no doubt in the minds of Anglican celebrants and congregations that the Service in which they are taking part, inasmuch as it is the fulfilment of Christ's command, is also expressive of His mind. But whether they are mistaken or not is a question for the New Testament scholar and theologian, and not for a student of liturgies. This question has been introduced by Mr. Smyth. He complains that I do not answer it, when it was not my concern to ask it. As he refrains from indicating how the question is to be answered, I can only conclude by noting that the evasion is not mine, but his.

2. PRINCIPLES GOVERNING LITURGICAL REFORM[1]

The range of this paper is necessarily limited by the general theme of the Congress. It is an Eucharistic Congress: accordingly we shall confine ourselves to considering the principles which should govern the reform of our Eucharistic Liturgy. Even thus circumscribed, the subject can hardly be exhausted in a single paper.

For several reasons, the subject is pressing. For one thing, some thirty years have elapsed since the appearance of the Alternative Communion Service of 1927-28. Chiefly on account of its Canon, that Service has been properly rejected by almost universal consent. Although no death certificate has yet been issued, the Service is indubitably dead. At the same time, the need for revision, which its compilers professed to meet, is as alive as ever it was half a century ago. Again, the rapid rise to popularity of the 'Parish Communion', and the consequent return of the Eucharistic Liturgy to its rightful place as the act of Sunday morning worship in very many churches, have revealed, in the rite of 1662, certain practical inadequacies which can be remedied only by the application of liturgical principles. Further, interest in liturgy is not nowadays restricted to a few professional scholars. It is spreading to a wider circle, and is shared by members of the laity, not least by students and other younger laymen, whom on becoming acquainted with the findings of such writers as Dom Gregory Dix[2], or Dr. Srawley[3], or Professor Jungman[4], are moved to ask why the new understanding of the history, principles and meaning of the Liturgy should not be brought to bear upon our own usage. In various degrees and modes, we see the influence of the new understanding at work in the liturgical reform and experiment now proceeding in the junior Churches of our Communion. Reform is in the Anglican air; and it is unlikely that the Church of England will continue indefinitely to postpone action in the matter. We must ask ourselves, then, by what principles we would wish to see our own liturgical revision governed; or (to put the question in another form) how can we apply the new understanding of the Liturgy to English usage?

There is a prolegomenary principle of basic importance. We have constantly to keep in mind the history, and particularly the early history, of the Liturgy and of its component parts. The reference to history is no mere antiquarianism. Only by tracing the history of an institution to its beginnings can we discover what its original structure and purpose were, and whether developments and modifications in its structure have either helped or hindered it in fulfilling its purpose. When, then, an institution is found to be in need of reform, we cannot properly restore it, or even perceive where its deformation lies, unless we have acquired some accurate knowledge of its beginnings and its history. If we neglect these, we run the risk of further deforming the institution; at best, we merely botch or tinker at it. The Eucharistic Liturgy is no exception to this rule.

1 [Address to the Eucharistic Congress sponsored by the Church Union, 1958. Reprinted in *The World for God,* the Congress papers (Church Literature Association, London), pp.64-72. For an introduction, see pp. 6-7 above.]

2 *The Shape of the Liturgy* (revised edition, 1954).

3 *The Early History of the Liturgy* (second edition, 1949).

4 *Missarum Sollemnia eine genetische Erklaerung der roemischen Messe* 1949, of which an English translation has been published under the title, *The Mass of the Roman Rite,* 2 vols., 1951-1955.

The usefulness of history appears at the outset of our enquiry. As everyone knows, the Liturgy is made up of two rites of 'Services' so closely conjoined as to present a unity. The first service is composed of Scripture lessons, sermon and prayers, with psalmody at the beginning and between the lessons: the second Service is the Eucharist itself. It will be convenient to take these two rites separately, and to begin, therefore, with the first. As we now have it, the first rite forms a generally appropriate, or not inappropriate, introduction to the second. Ought it to be something more? Has it a function of its own, independent of the rite which follows it? The question is relevant, because priests who have introduced the Parish Communion find themselves dissastisfied with the introductory rite of the Prayer Book Communion Service. They complain, in particular, that there is no obvious suitability in any of the appointed Epistles and Gospels. There is, indeed, a lack of unity and logic about the rite; and its patchwork quality is not relieved by a copious use of hymns. Historically, the first service was not intended to be a preparation for the second. It existed in its own right, and its function was to provide instruction. According to the earliest surviving description of it, it consisted of a Gospel or Prophetic lesson, followed by an instruction upon what had been read. It ended with 'common prayers' of an intercessory character. Such was the rite in the mid-second century, when Justin Martyr wrote his account of it.[1]

Not long after, we find an increase of lessons and the introduction of psalmody. In its developed form, the first Service was clearly an efficient instrument of instruction, well adjusted to the requirements of the early Christian communities. The sermon was related to the lessons. If Origen's homilies may be taken as an example of what the average preacher set out to do, but could not do so well, the early Christian congregation was soundly grounded in Biblical interpretation, in doctrine and in morals. If it had not been so grounded, we may be tempted to speculate whether the ancient Church would have won the ancient world for God; for, in the nature of things, the missionary work of the Church in the cities, towns and villages of the ancient world depended upon the local congregation, that is to say, upon the laity. The conditions of the modern church bear a certain resemblance to those of the ancient. We have become again a missionary society in our own land. We need a soundly instructed and an active, instead of a passive, laity. Why should not the first service recover its historic function of instruction? We are promised a revised selection of Epistles and Gospels designed to assist the parish priest in formulating a connected system of instruction for the Church's seasons. That will be a valuable reform. It could be still more valuable, if we were also to have, for reading before the Epistle on Sundays and certain feast days, a series of Old Testament lessons chosen for their pertinence to the Epistle or the Gospel, or to both. Further, the addition of carefully selected psalmody would greatly enhance the teaching value of the first rite. It would also bring in an element which Parish Communicants must lose to their disadvantage, unless they are disposed to attend Mattins. If we may not completely dispense with hymns, the psalmody could be confined to its traditional position between the lessons. The sermon, if it is to be (as it ought to be), not a pulpit chat, but an instruction based upon the lessons, would logically follow the Gospel. Probably, however, there would be

[1] *First Apology,* ch. 67.

little desire to change the position of the Creed; and if the Creed may be treated as a summary of the Faith set forth in the lessons, its present position is not inappropriate.

There remains the question of the intercession. In the rite of 1662, the General Prayer 'for the whole state of Christ's Church' is preceded by the setting of the alms and the elements upon the altar. This arrangement implies that the General Prayer is to be regarded as belonging to the second Service, that is, to the Eucharist itself. On the other hand, the rubric governing the practice known as 'Ante-Communion' plainly ranks the Prayer as a part of the first, in this way following ancient tradition; Ante-Communion is to end with the General Prayer, one or more collects and the blessing. There is plainly confusion here. It proceeds from imitation of the Scottish Liturgy of 1637, and we need not consider it further. It is enough to notice that the setting of the elements upon the altar, being the preliminary to their consecration, should not be included in the first Service[1]; whereas the General Prayer (as we shall notice) is not of the *esse* of the second.

In theory, the liturgical intercession is the solemn common or corporate prayer of the local Church. As such, it is appropriate and desirable on Sundays and other days when 'the most number of people come together'.[2] The form of the General Prayer, admirable as it is, scarcely fits it to discharge its true function. A litany, or a sequence of collects[3], would make it possible to insert petitions relating to current needs as occasion might require, and could restore actuality to the intercession. An expansion of the General Prayer would leave it inelastic.[4] Perhaps experiment alone could decide which form is best.

When we turn from the first Service to the second, we observe, or we ought to be able to observe, a difference as well as a distinction between them. It is a difference of direction. The first rite is one of *instruction,* in which primarily we receive; the second is a rite of *Worship,* in which primarily we give, or offer. If the first service is properly suited to its function, it will be an effectual introduction to the second. Christian worship is not an abstract lifting of the mind to the Supreme Being; it is homage and gratitude offered to God for his mighty acts recorded in the Scriptures. More particularly, it is homage and gratitude offered to him for the incarnation of his Son, and for the saving work which the Son was sent to do, and did. Christian worship therefore is characteristically thanksgiving, *Eucharistia,* and is pre-eminently the thanksgiving of the redeemed People of God, for the historical acts in which their redemption was achieved. Their worship is a remembrance. It is still less abstract even than that. Thanksgiving and remembrance can be expressed in a form of words, without action. The

---

1 This was recognized before 1662 by those Carolines whose custom it was (in want of direction in the Prayer Book) to set the elements on the Altar immediately before the Consecration Prayer: see *Hierurgia Anglicana,* revised edition, 1903, vol. II, pp.98, 239.

2 It is not indispensable for every day; and it should not be forgotten that the Offices, after the third collect, provide opportunity for intercession.

3 On the model of the Latin Good Friday Prayers.

4 The Alternative General Prayer of 1927-28 illustrated the failure of the method of expansion.

remembrance of the Christian Thanksgiving, on the other hand, is of a specific sort. It involves a concrete action with bread and a cup, and certain words, in imitation of the action and words of the Incarnate on the eve of his Passion. Hence, in a special manner, the Thanksgiving is a remembrance of his 'blessed' passion; it is equally a remembrance of his resurrection from the dead, because the resurrection discloses the redemptive power and meaning of the passion. Passion and resurrection are inseparable from each other. Again, because of its relation with what our Lord did and said on the eve of the passion, and consequently with the passion itself, the Thanksgiving is also a sacrifice, albeit an 'unbloody' sacrifice. We shall not understand why the early Church stressed the sacrifice, unless we recall how it took as applicable to itself the Deuteronomic commandment, 'Thou shalt not appear before the Lord thy God empty.'[1] Sacrifice is the appointed means of admission to the presence of God. What, then, is the Christian sacrifice? 'The passion is the Lord's sacrifice, and this we offer.' So wrote St. Cyprian with reference to the Eucharist; and his thought has run continuously through western eucharistic theology. Representing the Lord's passion with the bread and the cup, and (as it were) bearing it in their hands as their offering, for they have no other, the redeemed People of God appear, at the Eucharist, before the heavenly altar in the very presence of the Divine Majesty. Past and future become present; earth is joined with heaven; and for a moment, the Church on earth is united with the adoring company of the angels and the saints. The Eucharist, then, is the supreme occasion and act of the Church's worship 'reproducing visibly the Christian scheme of salvation',[2] as no singing of hymns and psalms, and no reading of lessons could do.

This understanding of early eucharistic worship has been recovered for us by modern study of the Liturgy. We cannot fail to be impressed by the objectivity of the worship. The attention of the worshippers, lifted up unto the Lord, is fixed upon Him and his acts. No less striking is the logically direct movement of the rite. The bread and cup are set before the celebrant. Immediately, he offers the Thanksgiving in a single, comprehensive prayer, which is, indeed, the one and only prayer of the rite, and which also (it may be added) is the ancestor of the later western Canon and eastern Anaphora. After the Thanksgiving the celebrant breaks the bread. The bread and the cup are then given in 'communion' to the worshippers who all partake of them. Thus the rite ends.[3] Its pattern and its logic are derived from the Institution: 'He took . . . He blessed . . . He brake . . . He gave.' In this pattern, a General Prayer is not in place. It was long before an intercession was interjected to break the sequence of communion upon Thanksgiving. It was long again before a prayer was attached to the end.

[1] [Ratcliff's manuscript (but not the printed text) has the note: 'The quotation is a translation of the LXX Greek Version, this being the version used by the early Christian writers.']

[2] Quoted from A. D. Nock, 'Early Gentile Christianity' in *Essays On The Trinity and the Incarnation,* ed. by A. E. J. Rawlinson, 1928, p.123.

[3] The early Eucharist can be reconstructed from Justin Martyr, *First Apology,* cc.65-67: for a summary of subsequent development see W. D. Maxwell, *An Outline of Christian Worship,* 1936, cc.I-III.

By comparison with the early rite, the second or Communion Service proper of the Prayer Book must appear, to many at least, unsatisfying. It has preserved the Institution pattern; but it has pulled it awry, and altered the proportion of its parts. It has broken the close relationship originally existing between the 'taking' of the elements and the 'blessing' or 'Thanksgiving'; and by whittling down the Thanksgiving to the minimum of the Preface, it has reduced the Thanksgiving to the status of an incidental. The emphasis of the English service falls upon the giving and taking of the bread and the cup in thankful remembrance of Christ's death. The resurrection is unnoticed, except in the Proper Prefaces of Easter and Ascension weeks. The most considerable part of the rite is to be found at the end. The post-Communion thanksgiving, both in content and dimension, exceeds what ought to be the substantive Thanksgiving, that is, the principal prayer of the rite. The want of proportion is disconcerting. We are often invited to admire the conclusion of the English Service. Its amplitude cannot be denied; but amplitude of tail is not normally held to counter-balance insufficieny of body.

In one other respect, we observe a difference from the early type of rite and worship. The English service sounds a strongly individualistic note. The intending communicant is not allowed to become unconscious of himself. The second half of the words of Administration demand of him the exercise of an intense personal piety of a kind not given to many. The exhortations and the Comfortable Words have already turned his attention inward upon himself, and have provoked questions and reflexions which (as we regard the matter nowadays) befit rather private preparation for worship than the corporate act of worship itself. We are probably mistaken, however, if we assume that the compilers of the service intended it to be a 'corporate act of worship' in the classical sense of the term.

What does our modern knowledge of liturgy suggest for the reform of the Service? The broad answer to this question has already been hinted. Let us restore to the Service the Institution pattern as the ancient rite adopted and adapted it, 'He took . . . He blessed . . . He brake . . . He gave,' i.e. Offertory, Thanksgiving (or Canon), Fraction, Communion. Let us restore the ancient proportion of the parts of the rite, so that the Thanksgiving is central and prominent. Let us restore these things, however, not because they are ancient but because they possess an innate fitness, which is proved, *inter alia*, by their resumption where they had been discontinued. They have been resumed, for example, in certain of the revised rites of the junior Anglican Churches and in the new rite of the Church of South India. Let us also recover, or attempt to recover, something of the objectivity of the ancient rite; again, not because it is ancient, but because objectivity is the most healthy climate for worship, and specially for corporate worship.

If these general principles were accepted, how would they be applied? Some attempt must be made to answer this question, although the present occasion does not permit a closely detailed answer.

As a preliminary, let us remove the Exhortations and the Comfortable Words to a 'Preparation' outside the complete Service. The Confession could properly be placed at the beginning of the complete service. A shorter formula, to be recited by ministers and people together, would be preferable.

If this usage were adopted, much of the material interposed between 'He took' and 'He blessed', that is, between the Offertory and the Thanksgiving, or Canon, would be withdrawn, without necessarily being lost.

The main revision affects each of the four points of the pattern. We may consider them in order.

If the nexus between the Offertory and Canon is to be re-established, the ceremony of placing the alms[1] and the elements upon the altar must be transferred to a new position after the General Prayer. We need a revision of the series of Offertory Sentences. In 1549, their purpose was to stimulate almsgiving. There is no evidence to suggest that they are particularly effective in that respect to-day. The South African Liturgy has shown how a return to the older usage in the matter of the Sentences could be made. If the alms and the elements are to be offered in a prayer at this point, let the offering be expressed in the plural 'we,' and not in the singular 'I' of the celebrant.[2] The celebrant has received the priesthood for exercise within the *Plebs sancta Dei,* and not apart from it. Where representatives of the people carry the alms and the elements in an 'Offertory Procession' to the sanctuary, only a plural prayer is appropriate.

The Thanksgiving, or Canon, which will follow immediately upon the Offertory, is in two parts. The first is the Preface, introduced with the traditional dialogue and ending with the Sanctus.

The second part continues and expands the thought of thanksgiving begun in the Preface; it enumerates the particular themes, creation and the incarnation, and so proceeds to the Consecration, which in turn is followed by the Anamnesis, or Remembrance of the Passion and Resurrection, and the Oblation. The Oblation could be used to bring in a reference to the heavenly altar; and the prayer could end with a petition that the worshippers be admitted to the fellowship of the Saints, thus closing upon a note which prepares the way for the Communion. The second part, although it gathers into one formula the dominant themes of the Eucharistic Action, and so by its greater length indicates its own importance, need not be as long as might be imagined or feared. The South African, Canadian and Indian revisions afford us examples of this type of prayer; another revision, the West Indian, is soon to appear. We could learn, both positively and negatively, from all of them. Two matters require short consideration. One is the title or description of the Canon. The traditional description, 'The Consecration', is a misnomer, Consecration being but one element among several. 'The Thanksgiving', or 'The Eucharistic Prayer',with the phrase, 'or Canon', as a sub-title, would be a correct description. The title should appear not after, but before the Preface. The other matter is the usage of Consecration. Let us firmly maintain our existing usage should attempts be renewed to alter it. Not only is that usage of long prescription in the Church of England; it is entirely sound in itself.

---

[1] We should not omit or depreciate the offering of money. Nowadays money is a more authentic offering than the elements, being the people's direct oblation of what is their own.

[2] E.g. 'Receive, O holy Father . . . this spotless host, which I thy unworthy servant do offer' etc., drawn from the Roman and other Latin Missals.

Of the Fraction, corresponding to 'He brake', little need be said, except that the breaking should be made after, not in, the Canon. The ceremony is a practical preliminary to the distribution whereby the 'many' are made partakers of 'that one bread'.[1] Whatever the convenience of individual unbroken wafers, they obscure the symbolism of the *Koinonia*, the 'communion' one with another, of which the communicants should be made aware in the rite. Could we not restore a larger type of wafer, the fraction of which would express the symbolism?

The Communion is the completion of the Eucharistic Action. Strictly considered, the Eucharistic Prayer is preparation enough for the Communion. At an early date in the West, however, the Lord's Prayer was introduced as a preliminary to reception, for which the clauses, 'Give us this day our daily bread' and 'Forgive us our trespasses, as we also forgive . . .' made it particularly appropriate.[2] The *Pax* fittingly links the Prayer with reception of the one bread and cup. We need no more preparation for communion than the Lord's Prayer and the Pax: but if the Prayer of Humble Access is to be retained within the rite[3], it would precede the Lord's Prayer.

There must be, of course, a Post-Communion. Let it be so called, and not 'The Thanksgiving', as though the Post-communion were itself the Eucharist! The present provision for the Post-communion is too strait. Could we not have a series of Post-communion prayers, of collect form, corresponding with the Collect of the Day? It would be an advantage to connect the Post-communion with Seasons and Festivals; and the sacramentaries which provided the majority of our collects could provide most of the Post-communion prayers. What of *Gloria in excelsis*? Here we tread on difficult ground. Many would prefer to keep it in its present position before the Blessing. On the other hand, there is no evident propriety in assigning it to the Post-communion. We may note, with interest, that in the new South Indian rite, whose compilers cannot be accused of blindly following in Latin paths, *Gloria in excelsis* occurs at the beginning of the complete Service. Finally let the rite close, and the people depart, with the Blessing, and with no Last Gospel to follow it. The end should be the end.

At length, this paper has come to its end. No one is more conscious of its defects than the author, who apologizes for them to his audience in the words which Cardinal Lothario wrote at the close of his treatise *De sacro mysterio altaris*, 'Feci diligenter ut potui, non sufficienter ut volui.'

---

1 I *Cor.,* 10, 17.
2 St. Cyprian, *De Oratione Dominica* c.18, notes the connexion between the Lord's Prayer and reception of the Eucharist. It is possible that the Prayer was originally said before private reception at home, and thence passed into the Liturgy.
3 It could be included in the 'Preparation' outside the complete Service.

3. A NOTE ON SCHEMES OF UNION, THE MINISTRY AND FORMS OF ORDINATION[1]

The Preface to the first English Book of Ordination Rites, or Ordinal, published in 1550, states it as 'evident' that 'from the Apostles' time there have been these Orders of Ministers in Christ's Church: Bishops, Priests and Deacons'; and proceeds to express the intention that these Orders should be continued in the now Reformed Church of England. The Preface was submitted to some enlargement in 1661, but the historical statement and the expression of intention were left unchanged. The practical effect of the latter was indeed enhanced by the new requirement, introduced because of the circumstances of the age, that, 'No man shall be accounted or taken to be a lawful Bishop, Priest or Deacon in the Church of England, or suffered to execute any of the said functions, except he be called, tried examined, and admitted thereunto according to the Form hereafter following, or hath had formerly Episcopal Consecration or Ordination'.

In the nature of things, the Preface ignores important matters of detail, e.g. the relation of the three Orders to the Apostolate, and the relation of the Presbyterate to the Episcopate. On the other hand, the Preface is incontestible evidence that at two decisive moments in its history, that is, at the inauguration and close of its reformation settlement, the Church of England was formally committed, by those who had power and authority to commit it, to the preservation of the 'historic' Ministry, and in particular to the 'historic' Episcopate. It is probable that the implications of the committal were not accepted by those responsible for the government of the Church of England in the reign of Edward IV. But the fact of the committal remained, and was made the subject of bitter complaint by the Puritans in the reign of Elizabeth I. The Episcopate was the principal target of Puritan attack. The objection against the Elizabethan Bishops that their name and office were 'drawne out of the Popes shop'[2], and that they themselves were 'Romish byshops, creatures of the Canon Law'[3], is the testimony of witnesses, qualified to judge, albeit hostile, to whom it appeared plain that the intention expressed in the Preface had been duly executed. Their opinion was later confirmed by Hooker's assertion that 'to be a bishop is now the self-same thing which it hath been'.[4] Arguing from a different standpoint, Roman Catholic controversialists set themselves, not to show (as we might have expected them to do) that the Church of England had established a new sort of episcopacy, but to prove that, for want of right consecration, the persons known as Bishops in the Church of England lacked the powers to perform episcopal functions.[5] The Roman Catholic controversialists did

---

[1] [Paper contributed by Professor E. C. Ratcliff at a conference of the Theological Committee [of The Church Union] on the Lambeth Unity Report, 7 January 1959. For an introduction to it, see pp.7-10 above.]

[2] *An Admonition to the Parliament*, 1572 (ed. Frere and Douglas, *Puritan Manifestoes*, Ch. Hist. Soc., 1907, p.30).

[3] *Certaine Articles* (1572-3), (Frere and Douglas, op. cit., p.138).

[4] *Ecclesiastical Polity*, VII, ii, 1.

[5] Cf. e.g. Harding's controversy with Jewel; Bristow's *Reply* to Fulke (1580); and Sanders's *De origine ac progressu Schismatis Anglicani* (1585)

not explicitly refer to the intention expressed in the Preface; nevertheless, in shaping their contentions so as to demonstrate that the intention had not been effectively executed, they obliquely witnessed to the intention itself.

These echoes of ancient controversy serve a useful purpose, if they remind us that the Anglican Communion is committed, by the early history of the reformed Church of England, to regarding its Ministry as the historic Ministry (i.e. not one Reformation ministry, of typically English conservative structure, among several); and to maintaining the historic Ministry, and particularly the Episcopate, in its integrity when entering into schemes of union, and assenting to Ordination Forms.

Nowadays it is unlikely that either of these positions would be repudiated in theory by any Church of the Anglican Communion. In practice, however, there is some danger that, either through failure to understand all the issues or out of charitable readiness to make the utmost concessions in schemes of union, Anglicans may be led to surrender some essential of the historic Episcopate and to assist in creating an Order of Ministry which, though named 'Bishops', is in fact something other than, or less than, the historic Episcopate. For instance, the Report of the Lambeth Committee on 'Church Unity and the Church Universal' states, 'Loyalty to the age-long tradition of the Church, and to our own experience, compels us to believe that a ministry to be acknowledged by every part of the Church can only be attained through the historic episcopate, though not necessarily in the precise form prevailing in any part of the Anglican Communion'.[1] The statement is admirable in general, but the qualifying clause, 'though not necessarily' etc. raises doubt. What measure of deviation from the Anglican norm can be considered as safely preserving the historic Episcopate? And at what point does deviation from the Anglican norm involve a loss of the historic Episcopate? We need a 'safety line' but none is drawn, and the matter is left open, probably to be settled by the practical expedient, 'Solvitur ambulando'. If reliance upon the expedient has so far produced satisfactory results, there is no assurance that it will continue to do so. At least some of the non-Anglicans invited to join with Anglicans in schemes of union are likely to ask the Anglicans to state the principles upon which the practical solution is founded. Recently, for example, a learned and prominent Wesleyan[2] Minister (who is not taking part in the present Anglican-Wesleyan Conversations, however), said in private conversation, 'You ask us to accept Bishops, but you do not tell us what a Bishop is. We know what he does, and the functions which he performs are provided for in our own ministry. What then is a Bishop, that we should be required to accept him?'

The question demands an answer. It is no answer to state that a Bishop is of supreme administrative convenience. He is not invariably such; and, in any case, Protestant churches can retort that their own ministries possess administrative conveniences adequate to their needs. An answer in practical terms misses the mark. Yet no other kind of answer is to be found in any official Anglican formulary. 'The Form of Ordaining or Consecrating

1 *The Lambeth Conference 1958* (S.P.C.K. London and Seabury, Greenwich, 1958) 2.22.
2 [Probably Dr. Robert Newton Flew (ed.)].

of an Archbishop or Bishop' contained in the Ordinal, for instance, expresses the Bishop's office in terms of function; teaching, preaching the Gospel, banishing erroneous doctrine, ordaining, governing. All these functions are proper to the historic Episcopate: but the Form suggests no reason why they should be so; and where the Greek and Latin Consecration Forms refer to *archierosune, summum Sacerdotium,* High-Priesthood, the English Form is silent. The silence is not difficult to understand in the light of the troubled conditions of the 16th century. Only practical measures were possible. Authority could prescribe what the Bishop should do; it could not prescribe any particular conception of him. Hooker's dictum, 'to be a bishop is now the selfsame thing which it hath been', is the nearest approach to an authoritative answer which Anglicans can make to the question, What is a Bishop? But Hooker's dictum is too summary. We need to investigate 'that which it hath been'. The investigation would inevitably lead us to the High-Priesthood, to Priesthood, to the question of Succession. The results of the investigation, however, would hardly win general assent within the Anglican Communion, as it now is. 'Catholics' would find the results generally acceptable; 'Protestants' would not. The results would scarcely commend themselves to the 'Free' churches. It is unlikely that, being aware of these possibilities, the present supreme authorities of the Anglican Communion would approve such an investigation, or would assent to its results, if it were undertaken. For the time, therefore, we must remain without an official answer to the question, and make the best of whatever embarassments lack of an answer, or rather of the correct answer, may entail. Until the Anglican Communion knows precisely what a Bishop is, and consequently knows what is his true relation to his Presbyters or Priests, and indeed to the church over which he presides, it cannot know for certain what deviations from the Anglican norm of Episcopacy are safe and permissible, and what are not.[1]

In another matter, equally important, the same Committee sounds an uncertain note. Under the sub-heading 'The Services for the Unification of the Ministry'[2], the Committee deals with the Forms of Ordination to be used when schemes of union have been effected. Much of what the Committee has to say will command agreement, and its expression of concern for the provision of a ministry 'fully accredited in the eyes . . . so far as may be of the Church throughout the world'[3] is right and commendable. The Committee's liturgical observations, on the other hand, are less fortunate; they suggest an unreconciled division of opinion as their background.

Anglicans have consistently maintained that the essential rite of Ordination to the Episcopate, the Presbyterate and the Diaconate, is prayer and the laying-on of hands. The Greco-Russian Orthodox concur in this opinion. Since the publication of the late Pope Pius XII's Apostolic Constitution, *Sacramentum Ordinis* (30 November 1947), the official interpretation of

[1] A move towards providing material for the historical aspects of the answer was made in the collection of essays entitled, *The Early History of the Church and the Ministry* (1918) edited by Prof. H. B. Swete at the instance of Abp. Randall Davidson.
[2] *The Lambeth Conference 1958* 2.36-3.8.
[3] *Idem* 2.36.

the Ordination Rites contained in the Pontifical has conformed with this opinion, without involving any modification or amendment of the Rites themselves. In theory, therefore, the historic Churches are in accord on this important matter. In liturgical practice, however, there are differences of such a character as to call for notice.

A comparative study of ancient Ordination Rites reveals a significant fact: Ordination was effected by laying-on of hands accompanied by the recitation of the Ordination Prayer, that is to say, the Ordination Prayer itself was the proper 'formula' for the laying-on of hands. The substantive clause of the Ordination Prayer was a petition asking God to send his Holy Spirit upon the person being ordained to make him a Bishop (or Priest or Deacon). This tradition is still maintained by the Greco-Russian Orthodox Church. The Greek rubric runs *'ho de archiereus echon ten cheira epikeim-enen euchetai houtos,'* the Prayer is then printed out. We can best describe this tradition in the phrase, Laying-on of hands *accompanied* by prayer.

The original Roman use was identical with that described above. At some time in the early middle age, the Pope adopted the practice of laying his hand in silence upon the head of each person being ordained to the Presbyterate,[1] and of saying the Ordination Prayer immediately afterwards. A similar usage was adopted at the Consecration of a Bishop. The Ordination of Priests was greatly elaborated during the middle age, and a second laying-on of hands was added at the end of the Ordination Mass. This second laying-on of hands was accompanied by the imperative formula, 'Accipe Spiritum Sanctum. Quorum remiseritis peccata' etc., and was counted the *essential* laying-on, the first and original imposition being ranked as a 'solemnity'. In the same way there was added to the originally silent laying of hands upon the Bishop the imperative formula 'Accipe Spiritum Sanctum'. The effect of *Sacramentum Ordinis* is to reconnect the laying-on of hands with the ancient Ordination Prayer proper to each Order, so that the laying-on of hands is the 'matter' and the substantive petition the 'form', of the Sacrament. Roman theory is now in substantial accord with the Greco-Russian. The Ordination Prayer determines the meaning of the laying-on of hands. Whatever the Rites might appear to suggest to the contrary, the essential act of Ordination is laying-on of hands with prayer.

When we turn to the Anglican Ordinal, we observe that the phrase, 'prayer and laying-on of hands' is interpreted liturgically to mean (a) Prayer *plus* (b) laying-on of hands accompanied by an imperative formula, so that the Prayer is separated from the laying-on of hands, and the meaning of the latter is interpreted by the imperative formula. Strictly considered, Anglican practice, as distinct from Anglican theory, suggests that the essence of Ordination consists of laying-on of hands accompanied by a formula in which the Order is conferred. Anglican practice thus retains the mediaeval tradition; and it is not surprising that, when entering into negotiations for union, Anglicans desire the Services for 'Unification of Ministries' to follow the (a) *plus* (b) pattern of their own Ordinal, while being agreeable to a re-phrasing of the formula of (b). The desirability of perpetuating the (a) *plus* (b) pattern is highly doubtful, particularly when it is employed for the

1 Possibly because the number of candidates made the older practice inconvenient.

establishment of a Ministry 'to be acknowledged by every part of the Church'. When it is perpetuated, great care is required in phrasing the formula of (b).

Commenting on the adaptation of the (a) plus (b) pattern to 'Unification, Services in general, the Committee remarks that 'Wherever it is possible, it is *desirable* that in the Prayer (as well as in the Formula) the specific office or Order of Ministry in view should be named'. About the form of the Formula the Committee says nothing; it limits itself to the content, suggesting that it will refer to 'the grace and authority of Ministry in the Church of God, which each brings and which is to be continued and enriched by means of the Prayer, the laying-on of hands, and the Formula', and to 'the conferring of authority and jurisdiction within the local Church'.[1] The confused character of these comments is plain. If the Prayer is a constituent of the Ordination, it is more than merely 'desirable' that the Order in view should be named. Again, if the Committee's comments were taken as a guide for the drawing up of a Formula, it would be possible, and easy, to frame one which would fall short of determining the meaning of the laying-on of hands in a Catholic or historic sense. Further, if there is some special necessity for conferring authority and jurisdiction within the local Church, the formula for conferring them should be distinct from that accompanying the laying-on of hands. That the Committee's ideas on this matter lack clarity is shown by its approval, for the North India-Pakistan Unification Service, of an optative form for the Formula, '. . . mayst thou receive . . .'[2], apparently for Presbyters only. An optative Formula is no more than a pious aspiration. It cannot be regarded as conferring an Order. It is of no more force than the Bishop's words, 'Almighty God . . . grant also unto you strength and power' etc., addressed to the candidates for Priesthood at the end of the questions in the Anglican Ordinal. No one presumably would contend that strength and power are conferred by this formula. If the Committee had been unable to recommend the uniting of the laying-on of hands with the Prayer, in conformity with the historic tradition, it would have been wiser, had it proposed the retention of the Anglican imperative formula, 'Receive the Holy Ghost', for which (distasteful as it may be to the negotiating churches) the authority of John 20.22f. may be alleged. As the Rite for North India-Pakistan Unification of Ministries now stands, even if revised in accordance with the Committee's recommendations, it cannot be considered as sufficient for Ordination to the historic Ministry.

In conclusion, it may be permitted to recall how the historic Ordination Rites conceive Ordinations to be effected:

(i)   Ministers are made, not by the Bishop, but by God, the Father or the Son;

(ii)   God makes Ministers by giving them, at the prayer of the Church, His Holy Spirit to furnish them with grace for their particular Ministry;

(iii)   The role of the Bishop is that of intermediary or agent. He is (a) the intermediary for his Church when he presents candidates to God, in

---

[1] *The Lambeth Conference 1958*, 2.37f.
[2] *Idem.* 2.40.

the Prayer for God's action upon them with His Spirit; and (b) the intermediary for God when he lays his hands, at the Prayer, upon the candidates, the action being understood by the Church as God's method of bestowing His Spirit.

(iv) It may be added that, in so acting, the Bishop is seen to be the *archiereus,* the Summus Sacerdos, the High Priest, of the local Church.

Much more might be said about the background. But upon these points the ancient Rites are agreed; hence their testimony to laying-on of hands accompanied by prayer as the essential of Ordination. Neglect or ignorance of these points has led to most of our troubles.